Understanding

VIAGRA

A Comprehensive Guide to Understanding and Safely Using Viagra

Nicholas Baker

Titolo | Understanding VIAGRA - A Comprehensive Guide to Understanding and Safely Using Viagra
Autore | Nicholas Baker
ISBN | 979-12-22758-26-8

Youcanprint
Via Marco Biagi 6, 73100 Lecce
www.youcanprint.it

Legal Disclaimer

The information provided in this book, "Understanding VIAGRA" is for general informational and educational purposes only. The author, Nicholas Baker, is not a licensed medical professional, and the content should not be considered a substitute for professional medical advice, diagnosis, or treatment.

Readers are encouraged to consult with their healthcare provider or a qualified medical professional before engaging in any intake of drugs, especially if they have pre-existing health conditions or concerns.

Table of Content

Chapter 1: Introduction to Viagra – History and Development

What is Viagra?

Viagra, known generically as sildenafil citrate, is a medication primarily used to treat erectile dysfunction (ED) in men. Erectile dysfunction is the inability to achieve or maintain an erection sufficient for satisfactory sexual performance. Viagra helps by increasing blood flow to the penis, which aids in achieving and sustaining an erection when combined with sexual stimulation.

The Discovery and Development of Viagra

The journey of Viagra began in the late 1980s with a group of scientists at Pfizer, a major pharmaceutical company. Originally, sildenafil citrate was synthesized with the hope of treating hypertension (high blood pressure) and angina pectoris (a type of chest pain associated with coronary heart disease).

During clinical trials, researchers observed an interesting side effect: many male participants reported experiencing improved erections. This unexpected outcome redirected the focus of research. Recognizing the potential, Pfizer began investigating sildenafil citrate as a treatment for erectile dysfunction.

Approval and Introduction to the Market

After extensive testing and clinical trials, Viagra was approved by the U.S. Food and Drug Administration (FDA) on March 27, 1998. It became the first oral treatment for erectile dysfunction to be approved in the United States. The approval was a landmark moment in medicine, offering a convenient and effective treatment for millions of men worldwide.

Viagra's introduction revolutionized the approach to treating erectile dysfunction. Prior to Viagra, treatments included penile injections, vacuum erection devices, and surgical implants, which were often invasive, uncomfortable, and less accepted by patients.

How Viagra Works: The Science behind the Pill

To understand how Viagra works, it is essential to grasp some basic physiology. An erection involves a complex interplay of psychological, neural, vascular, and hormonal factors. When a man is sexually stimulated, the brain sends signals to the nerves in the penis. These nerves release a chemical called nitric oxide, which stimulates the production of another molecule called cyclic guanosine monophosphate (cGMP).

cGMP causes the smooth muscles in the walls of the penile arteries to relax, allowing blood to flow into the spongy tissue of the penis (corpora cavernosa), resulting in an erection. After sexual activity, another enzyme called phosphodiesterase type 5 (PDE5) breaks down cGMP, causing the erection to subside.

Viagra works by inhibiting PDE5, thereby preventing the breakdown of cGMP. This prolongs the muscle relaxation and increases blood flow to the penis, facilitating an erection in response to sexual stimulation.

The Impact of Viagra on Society and Medicine

The introduction of Viagra had profound effects not only on the treatment of erectile dysfunction but also on societal attitudes towards sexual health. Erectile dysfunction, once a taboo subject, became a topic of open discussion, reducing stigma and encouraging men to seek help for their condition.

Viagra also spurred further research and development in the field of sexual medicine. Its success prompted the development of other PDE5 inhibitors, such as tadalafil (Cialis) and vardenafil (Levitra), offering more options to men suffering from ED.

The Evolution of Viagra

Since its launch, Viagra has undergone various changes, including the introduction of generic versions and the development of different formulations. Initially available only in a blue, diamond-shaped pill, sildenafil is now available in various forms, including orally disintegrating tablets and chewable forms, to enhance convenience and accessibility.

In addition to its use in treating erectile dysfunction, sildenafil has been investigated and approved for other medical conditions. For example, a formulation called Revatio is used to treat pulmonary arterial hypertension (PAH), a type of high blood pressure that affects the arteries in the lungs.

Viagra's history is a remarkable tale of scientific discovery, serendipity, and societal impact. From its initial development as a heart medication to becoming a groundbreaking treatment for erectile dysfunction, Viagra has transformed the lives of millions of men and their partners. Understanding the history and development of Viagra provides a foundation for appreciating its role in modern medicine and sexual health.

We will delve deeper into the medical background of erectile dysfunction, how Viagra works at a molecular level, guidelines for safe usage, and much more. This comprehensive guide aims to equip you with all the information needed for the safe and informed use of Viagra.

Common Myths and Misconceptions about Viagra

Viagra, like many breakthrough medications, has become the subject of various myths and misconceptions since its introduction. Addressing these misconceptions is crucial for understanding the drug's true benefits and limitations. While we'll explore these myths in more detail in later chapters, here are some common misconceptions about Viagra:

Myth 1: Viagra is an Aphrodisiac

Reality: Many people mistakenly believe that Viagra acts as an aphrodisiac, directly increasing sexual desire. In reality, Viagra does not affect sexual desire or libido. It works by facilitating the physical process of achieving an erection in response to sexual stimulation. Without arousal, Viagra will not cause an erection.

Myth 2: Viagra Works Instantly

Reality: Another common misconception is that Viagra produces an immediate erection upon ingestion. In truth, Viagra typically takes about 30 to 60 minutes to start working and requires sexual stimulation to be effective. The timing can vary based on factors such as food intake, overall health, and other medications being taken.

Myth 3: Viagra is Only for Older Men

Reality: While erectile dysfunction is more prevalent among older men, younger men can also experience ED due to various factors such as stress, anxiety, or medical conditions. Viagra can be prescribed to men of different age groups who have been diagnosed with erectile dysfunction.

Myth 4: Taking More Viagra Will Improve Its Effectiveness

Reality: Some believe that taking a higher dose of Viagra will produce better results. However, increasing the dosage can lead to a higher risk of side effects without necessarily improving effectiveness. It is important to follow the prescribed dosage and consult a healthcare provider for any adjustments.

Myth 5: Viagra Can Be Used Recreationally Without Risks

Reality: Using Viagra without a medical need or prescription can be dangerous. Recreational use can lead to serious health risks, including cardiovascular problems. Additionally, using Viagra in combination with certain substances, such as alcohol or illicit drugs, can have harmful interactions.

Myth 6: Viagra is Addictive

Reality: Viagra is not addictive and does not cause physical dependence. However, psychological dependence can develop if individuals come to rely on the medication for confidence in sexual performance. It is essential to address underlying psychological or relational issues that may contribute to ED.

Myth 7: Viagra Fixes All Types of Erectile Dysfunction

Reality: While Viagra is effective for many men with ED, it may not work for everyone. Some types of erectile dysfunction, particularly those caused by severe nerve damage or hormonal imbalances, may not respond well to PDE5 inhibitors like Viagra. Alternative treatments may be necessary for these cases.

By addressing these myths and misconceptions, we aim to provide a clearer understanding of what Viagra can and cannot do. In the following chapters, we will delve deeper into these topics, providing comprehensive insights and debunking false beliefs to ensure safe and informed use of the medication.

Chapter 2: Medical Background

Understanding Erectile Dysfunction (ED)

Erectile Dysfunction (ED) is the inability to achieve or maintain an erection sufficient for satisfactory sexual performance. It is a common condition that affects men of all ages but becomes more prevalent with increasing age. ED can have a significant impact on a man's self-esteem, relationships, and overall quality of life.

An erection is a complex physiological process involving the brain, nerves, hormones, muscles, and blood circulation. When a man is sexually stimulated, the brain sends signals to the nerves in the penis. These nerves release chemicals that increase blood flow into the penis, causing it to become erect. Any disruption in this process can result in erectile dysfunction.

Causes and Prevalence of ED

Prevalence of ED:

Erectile dysfunction is a widespread issue, affecting an estimated 30 million men in the United States alone. According to the Massachusetts Male Aging Study, approximately 52% of men between the ages of 40 and 70 experience some form of ED. The prevalence increases with age, with about 40% of men at age 40 and nearly 70% of men at age 70 experiencing ED.

Causes of ED:

The causes of erectile dysfunction can be broadly categorized into physical (organic) and psychological factors. Often, ED results from a combination of both.

Physical Causes

Physical health is equally important in maintaining erectile function. Several physiological aspects can influence ED:

Cardiovascular Diseases: Healthy blood flow is crucial for an erection. Conditions such as hypertension (high blood pressure), atherosclerosis (hardening of the arteries), and high cholesterol can impair blood flow to the penis, leading to ED.

Diabetes: Diabetes can damage blood vessels and nerves that control erections, making it a significant risk factor for ED.

Neurological Disorders: Nerve signals from the brain trigger the release of chemicals that cause the penile arteries to dilate.

Conditions like Parkinson's disease, multiple sclerosis, and spinal cord injuries can disrupt nerve signals between the brain and the penis.

Hormonal balances: Hormones such as testosterone play a vital role in sexual desire and erectile function. Hormonal imbalances, including low testosterone levels, can lead to ED.

Medications: Some medications, including antidepressants, antihypertensives, and certain cancer treatments, can cause erectile dysfunction as a side effect.

Lifestyle Factors: Smoking, excessive alcohol consumption, lack of physical activity, and obesity can all contribute to the development of ED.

Muscle Function: The smooth muscles in the penis need to relax to allow blood flow for an erection. Conditions that affect these muscles can cause ED.

Peyronie's Disease: This condition, characterized by the development of fibrous scar tissue inside the penis, can lead to painful erections and ED.

Psychological Causes:

Psychological factors play a crucial role in sexual health and can independently cause or exacerbate ED. The mind and body are closely interconnected, and mental health significantly affects sexual performance.

Stress and Anxiety: Performance anxiety, stress about sexual performance, and general stress can interfere with sexual arousal and erections. Fear of not being able to achieve or maintain an erection can create a self-fulfilling prophecy, leading to repeated instances of ED.

Depression: Depression can decrease libido and result in ED. Additionally, some antidepressant medications can contribute to ED. Depression not only reduces sexual interest but can also disrupt the physiological processes involved in erections.

Relationship Issues: Poor communication, unresolved conflicts, and lack of intimacy can affect sexual function.

Psychological Trauma: Past experiences, including sexual abuse or traumatic events, can impact sexual health and lead to ED.

By understanding the medical background of erectile dysfunction, including its causes and contributing factors, we can better appreciate the role of treatments like Viagra.

Chapter 3: Mechanism of Action

Pharmacodynamics and Pharmacokinetics

Pharmacodynamics:

Pharmacodynamics refers to how a drug affects the body. Viagra's primary active ingredient, sildenafil citrate, is classified as a phosphodiesterase type 5 (PDE5) inhibitor. PDE5 is an enzyme found in various tissues, including the smooth muscle cells lining the blood vessels of the penis.

Viagra works by inhibiting PDE5, preventing it from breaking down cyclic guanosine monophosphate (cGMP). cGMP is a crucial molecule that regulates blood flow in the penis. By blocking PDE5, Viagra increases the levels of cGMP, promoting relaxation of smooth muscle cells and enhancing blood flow into the penile tissues during sexual stimulation, leading to an erection.

Pharmacokinetics:

Pharmacokinetics describes how the body absorbs, distributes, metabolizes, and excretes a drug.

- *Absorption:* After oral ingestion, Viagra is rapidly absorbed, reaching peak plasma concentrations within 30 to 120 minutes. It is best taken on an empty stomach, as high-fat meals can delay its absorption and reduce its effectiveness.

- *Distribution*: Viagra is distributed throughout the body, binding to plasma proteins at a rate of about 96%. It primarily acts on the penile tissues but can affect other areas with smooth muscle cells.

- *Metabolism*: The liver metabolizes Viagra, primarily through the cytochrome P450 enzymes CYP3A4 and CYP2C9. The main metabolite, N-desmethylated sildenafil, also has some PDE5 inhibitory activity but to a lesser extent than the parent compound.

- *Excretion:* The drug and its metabolites are primarily excreted in the feces (approximately 80%) and to a lesser extent in the urine (about 13%). The terminal half-life of

Viagra is around 4 hours, meaning its effects gradually diminish after this period.

The Role of Nitric Oxide and cGMP

Nitric Oxide (NO):

Nitric oxide is a key molecule in the process of achieving an erection. Sexual stimulation triggers the release of NO from nerve endings and endothelial cells (cells lining the blood vessels) in the penis. NO activates an enzyme called guanylate cyclase, which increases the production of cGMP from guanosine triphosphate (GTP).

cGMP (Cyclic Guanosine Monophosphate):

cGMP is a signaling molecule that causes the smooth muscle cells in the walls of the penile blood vessels to relax. This relaxation dilates the blood vessels, allowing more blood to flow into the corpora cavernosa, the spongy tissue of the penis. As the corpora cavernosa fills with blood, the penis becomes engorged and erect.

How Viagra Enhances Blood Flow

Inhibition of PDE5:

Under normal conditions, PDE5 breaks down cGMP, regulating blood flow by ensuring that the smooth muscle cells return to their contracted state after sexual activity. In men with erectile dysfunction, this regulation is often disrupted, leading to insufficient blood flow and difficulty achieving or maintaining an erection.

Viagra enhances blood flow to the penis by inhibiting PDE5, which prevents the breakdown of cGMP. As a result, cGMP levels remain elevated for a longer period, promoting sustained relaxation of the smooth muscle cells and increased blood flow into the penis during sexual stimulation.

Mechanism in Detail:

- *Sexual Stimulation*: Sexual arousal activates the release of nitric oxide (NO) in the penile tissues.
- *NO Release*: NO stimulates the enzyme guanylate cyclase, increasing the levels of cGMP.
- *cGMP Action*: Elevated cGMP causes the smooth muscle cells in the penile blood vessels to relax, leading to

vasodilation and increased blood flow into the corpora cavernosa.

- *Erection*: The engorgement of the corpora cavernosa with blood results in an erection.
- *Viagra's Role*: By inhibiting PDE5, Viagra ensures that cGMP is not broken down prematurely, maintaining its concentration and prolonging the erection.

Effectiveness and Duration:

Viagra is effective in achieving erections for most men with ED, provided there is sexual stimulation. Its effects typically begin within 30 to 60 minutes and can last for up to 4 hours. However, the duration of action can vary based on individual factors such as age, metabolism, and overall health.

In summary, Viagra's mechanism of action involves enhancing the natural process of erection by inhibiting PDE5 and maintaining elevated levels of cGMP. This facilitates improved blood flow to the penis during sexual arousal, helping men with erectile dysfunction achieve and sustain erections.

Chapter 4: Usage Guidelines

Indications for Use

Erectile Dysfunction (ED):

Viagra is primarily indicated for the treatment of erectile dysfunction (ED) in men. ED is the inability to achieve or maintain an erection sufficient for satisfactory sexual performance. It can result from various physical, psychological, or lifestyle factors. Viagra helps men with ED by enhancing the natural erectile response to sexual stimulation.

Pulmonary Arterial Hypertension (PAH):

A different formulation of sildenafil (under the brand name Revatio) is indicated for the treatment of pulmonary arterial hypertension (PAH). PAH is a condition characterized by high blood pressure in the arteries that supply the lungs. It leads to symptoms such as shortness of breath, dizziness, and fatigue.

Sildenafil helps relax the blood vessels in the lungs, reducing the workload on the heart.

Dosage Information

Standard Dosage:

For the treatment of erectile dysfunction, the typical starting dose of Viagra for most men is 50 mg, taken as needed approximately one hour before sexual activity. However, the dose can be adjusted based on efficacy and tolerability. The maximum recommended dosing frequency is once per day.

Dosage Adjustments:

- *Increase:* If the 50 mg dose is not effective, the doctor may increase the dose to a maximum of 100 mg.
- *Decrease*: If side effects are bothersome or the 50 mg dose is too strong, the doctor may reduce the dose to 25 mg.

Special Populations:

- *Older Adults*: Men over the age of 65 may start with a lower dose, such as 25 mg, due to slower metabolism and increased sensitivity to the drug.
- *Hepatic Impairment*: Patients with liver problems may require dosage adjustments.

- *Renal Impairment*: Men with kidney issues may also need lower doses, especially if they have severe renal impairment.

How to Take Viagra Correctly

Timing:

- Viagra should be taken about 30 to 60 minutes before sexual activity.
- It can be taken up to 4 hours before sexual activity, providing a flexible window for use.
- Sexual stimulation is necessary for Viagra to work; it will not cause an erection just by taking the pill.

With or Without Food:

- Viagra can be taken with or without food.
- However, taking it with a high-fat meal may delay its onset of action. For faster effectiveness, it is best to take Viagra on an empty stomach.

Administration:

- Swallow the tablet whole with a glass of water.
- Do not split, crush, or chew the tablet, as this can affect its effectiveness.

Avoiding Interactions:

- *Alcohol*: Limit alcohol consumption when taking Viagra, as excessive drinking can increase the risk of side effects and impair the ability to get an erection.
- *Grapefruit Juice*: Avoid grapefruit and grapefruit juice, as they can increase sildenafil levels in the blood and raise the risk of side effects.
- *Other Medications*: Inform your healthcare provider about all medications you are taking, including prescription, over-the-counter, herbal supplements, and recreational drugs. Certain medications, especially nitrates (used for chest pain) and alpha-blockers (used for high blood pressure or prostate issues), can cause dangerous interactions with Viagra.

Missed Dose:

- Viagra is taken as needed, so there is no dosing schedule. If you miss a dose for an anticipated sexual activity, take it as soon as you remember. Do not take more than one dose per day.

Storage:

- Store Viagra at room temperature away from moisture and heat. Keep it out of reach of children and pets.

Important Considerations:

- Consultation with Healthcare Provider: Always consult a healthcare provider before starting Viagra to ensure it is appropriate for your condition and to discuss potential risks and benefits.

- Monitoring: Regular follow-ups with your healthcare provider are important to monitor the effectiveness and any side effects of the medication.
- Lifestyle Modifications: Combining Viagra with healthy lifestyle changes, such as regular exercise, a balanced diet, quitting smoking, and reducing alcohol intake, can enhance its effectiveness and improve overall sexual health.

By following these usage guidelines, you can maximize the benefits of Viagra while minimizing the risk of side effects and complications. In the next chapters, we will explore the safety profile of Viagra, including common and serious side effects, drug interactions, and precautions for specific populations.

Chapter 5: Safety and Side Effects

Common Side Effects

While Viagra is generally well-tolerated, it can cause some common side effects. These side effects are usually mild to moderate and often diminish as the body adjusts to the medication.

Common Side Effects Include:

- *Headache:* This is the most frequently reported side effect, experienced by about 16% of users.
- *Flushing:* Many men experience a warm sensation or redness in the face, neck, or chest.
- *Indigestion:* Also known as dyspepsia, this can include symptoms like stomach discomfort, bloating, and nausea.
- *Nasal Congestion*: A stuffy or runny nose is a common side effect.

- *Dizziness:* Some users may feel lightheaded or dizzy, especially when standing up quickly.
- *Visual Disturbances*: Changes in color vision, blurred vision, or sensitivity to light may occur. This happens because sildenafil affects PDE6, an enzyme found in the retina.
- *Muscle Pain (Myalgia)*: Some men may experience muscle aches or back pain.

Serious Adverse Reactions

Though rare, Viagra can cause serious adverse reactions. These require immediate medical attention.

Serious Adverse Reactions Include:

- *Priapism*: A prolonged and painful erection lasting more than 4 hours. This condition can cause permanent damage to the penis if not treated promptly.
- *Sudden Vision Loss*: A rare condition called non-arteritic anterior ischemic optic neuropathy (NAION) can lead to sudden vision loss in one or both eyes.
- *Hearing Loss*: Sudden decrease or loss of hearing has been reported, sometimes accompanied by tinnitus (ringing in the ears) and dizziness.

- *Severe Allergic Reactions*: Symptoms such as rash, itching/swelling (especially of the face/tongue/throat), severe dizziness, and trouble breathing may indicate a serious allergic reaction.
- *Heart Attack or Stroke:* Men with preexisting cardiovascular conditions may be at higher risk. Symptoms include chest pain, shortness of breath, irregular heartbeat, and pain spreading to the arm or shoulder.

Drug Interactions and Contraindications

Drug Interactions:

Viagra can interact with other medications, potentially leading to harmful effects. It is crucial to inform your healthcare provider about all medications and supplements you are taking.

- *Nitrates*: Concurrent use with nitrates (e.g., nitroglycerin, isosorbide dinitrate) can cause a severe drop in blood pressure, leading to fainting, stroke, or heart attack. This interaction is a significant contraindication.
- *Alpha-Blockers*: Used for high blood pressure or prostate problems, these can also cause a significant drop in blood pressure when taken with Viagra.
- *Protease Inhibitors*: Used for HIV treatment, such as ritonavir, can increase sildenafil levels in the blood, increasing the risk of side effects.

- *Other PDE5 Inhibitors*: Combining Viagra with other PDE5 inhibitors or similar medications for ED or PAH can increase the risk of adverse effects.
- *Antifungals and Antibiotics*: Medications like ketoconazole, itraconazole, erythromycin, and clarithromycin can increase sildenafil levels in the blood.
- *Blood Thinners*: Warfarin and other anticoagulants can interact with Viagra, increasing the risk of bleeding.

Contraindications:

Certain conditions make Viagra unsafe for some individuals.

- *Severe Cardiovascular Disorders*: Patients with severe heart disease, recent history of heart attack or stroke, or those advised against sexual activity should not take Viagra.
- *Severe Liver Impairment*: Men with severe liver problems should avoid Viagra.
- *Kidney Disease*: Severe renal impairment may necessitate dosage adjustments or avoidance of Viagra.
- *Hypotension*: Those with low blood pressure (below 90/50 mmHg) should not take Viagra.
- *Retinitis Pigmentosa*: A rare genetic disorder of the retina, patients with this condition should avoid PDE5 inhibitors.

Precautions and Warnings

Precautions:

- *Medical History*: Always provide a complete medical history to your healthcare provider, including heart problems, high or low blood pressure, stroke, liver or kidney disease, eye conditions, bleeding disorders, and stomach ulcers.
- *Alcohol:* Limit alcohol consumption, as it can increase the risk of side effects like dizziness, headache, and low blood pressure.
- *Driving and Operating Machinery*: Viagra can cause dizziness and visual disturbances. Do not drive or operate heavy machinery until you know how the medication affects you.
- *Grapefruit Juice*: Avoid grapefruit juice, as it can interfere with the metabolism of sildenafil and increase the risk of side effects.
- *Pregnancy and Breastfeeding*: Viagra is not indicated for use in women. The effects of Viagra in pregnant or breastfeeding women have not been studied, and it should not be used unless clearly needed and prescribed by a healthcare provider.

Warnings:

- *Cardiovascular Risk*: Viagra has systemic vasodilatory properties that can result in transient decreases in blood pressure. Use with caution in patients with underlying cardiovascular disease.

- *Priapism:* Seek immediate medical help for erections lasting more than 4 hours to prevent permanent damage.
- *Visual and Auditory Issues*: If you experience sudden vision or hearing loss, stop taking Viagra and seek immediate medical attention.
- *Interaction with Recreational Drugs*: Avoid using Viagra with recreational drugs, particularly those known as "poppers" (amyl nitrate or nitrite), as this can cause severe drops in blood pressure.

By understanding the safety profile and potential side effects of Viagra, you can use the medication responsibly and effectively. Always follow the guidance of your healthcare provider and report any unusual or severe reactions promptly.

Chapter 6: Who Should Not Take Viagra

Viagra can be an effective treatment for erectile dysfunction (ED), but it is not suitable for everyone. Certain health conditions and risk factors can make its use unsafe, potentially leading to serious side effects. This chapter explores the health conditions that contraindicate Viagra use and highlights the risk factors that may increase the likelihood of adverse effects.

Health Conditions That Contraindicate Use

Cardiovascular Disorders

1. *Severe Heart Disease*: Individuals with severe heart conditions, such as heart failure or unstable angina, should avoid Viagra. The drug's vasodilatory effects can lower

blood pressure, which may be dangerous for those with compromised heart function.

2. *Recent Heart Attack or Stroke*: Men who have recently experienced a heart attack or stroke should not use Viagra until cleared by a healthcare provider. The stress of sexual activity, combined with the effects of Viagra, could increase the risk of another cardiovascular event.
3. *Arrhythmias*: Men with serious irregular heart rhythms should be cautious with Viagra, as changes in blood pressure can exacerbate these conditions.

Low Blood Pressure (Hypotension)

Viagra can further lower blood pressure, posing risks to individuals with already low blood pressure (below 90/50 mmHg). This can lead to dizziness, fainting, or even shock.

Retinitis Pigmentosa

This rare genetic disorder affects the retina, and some forms are associated with PDE5 enzyme abnormalities. Patients with retinitis pigmentosa should avoid Viagra, as it could potentially worsen their vision condition.

Severe Liver Impairment

The liver metabolizes Viagra, so severe liver disease can lead to higher levels of the drug in the bloodstream, increasing the risk of side effects. Men with severe liver impairment should generally avoid Viagra.

Severe Renal Impairment

Similarly, severe kidney problems can lead to accumulation of Viagra in the body. Dosage adjustments may be necessary for those with significant renal impairment, but severe cases should avoid use altogether.

Anatomical Deformities of the Penis

Conditions such as Peyronie's disease (curvature of the penis due to scar tissue) can be exacerbated by Viagra. The increased blood flow and erection pressure may cause injury or worsening of the condition.

Risk Factors for Adverse Effects

Certain risk factors can increase the likelihood of adverse effects when taking Viagra. Individuals with these risk factors should use Viagra cautiously and under the guidance of a healthcare provider.

Age

Older adults may have an increased risk of side effects due to age-related changes in drug metabolism and clearance. They may require lower doses to achieve the desired effect safely.

Concurrent Medication Use

- *Nitrates*: Concurrent use of nitrates for chest pain or heart disease with Viagra is contraindicated due to the risk of a severe drop in blood pressure.
- *Alpha-Blockers*: These medications, often used for hypertension or prostate issues, can also lower blood pressure and interact with Viagra, increasing the risk of hypotension.
- *Other PDE5 Inhibitors*: Combining Viagra with other drugs of the same class or similar medications used to treat PAH can lead to increased side effects.

Lifestyle Factors

- *Smoking*: Smoking can exacerbate cardiovascular risks and reduce the effectiveness of Viagra. Smokers may experience more severe side effects and should consider cessation programs.
- *Excessive Alcohol Consumption*: Alcohol can increase the risk of side effects like dizziness and fainting, as well as decrease the effectiveness of Viagra.

Psychological Conditions

- *Depression and Anxiety*: These conditions can contribute to erectile dysfunction and may affect the overall effectiveness of Viagra. Additionally, some antidepressant medications can interact with Viagra.
- *Psychological Dependence*: Some individuals may develop a psychological reliance on Viagra for confidence in sexual performance, which can impact their natural erectile function.

Hypersensitivity

Individuals with a known allergy or hypersensitivity to sildenafil or any of the inactive ingredients in Viagra should not take the medication. Signs of an allergic reaction include rash, itching/swelling, severe dizziness, and difficulty breathing.

Monitoring and Consultation

Individuals considering Viagra should have a thorough consultation with a healthcare provider to evaluate their health status and determine if Viagra is appropriate for them. Regular follow-ups can help monitor the drug's effectiveness and any potential side effects.

Understanding who should not take Viagra is crucial to ensure safe and effective use of the medication.

Chapter 7: Viagra and Other ED Treatments

Erectile dysfunction (ED) is a common condition that can significantly affect quality of life. Fortunately, various treatment options are available to help men manage this condition. This chapter explores how Viagra compares with other ED medications, discusses alternative therapies and lifestyle changes, and examines the potential benefits of combination therapies.

Comparison with Other ED Medications

Viagra is one of several medications used to treat erectile dysfunction. It belongs to a class of drugs known as phosphodiesterase type 5 (PDE5) inhibitors. While Viagra is perhaps the most well-known, other PDE5 inhibitors are also available.

Sildenafil (Viagra)

Onset and Duration: Typically works within 30 to 60 minutes, with effects lasting about 4 hours.

Dosage Forms: Available in 25 mg, 50 mg, and 100 mg tablets.

Best For: Situations where planned sexual activity is expected and timing is flexible.

Tadalafil (Cialis)

- *Onset and Duration*: Can work as quickly as 15 to 30 minutes and lasts up to 36 hours. This extended duration is why it's often called the "weekend pill."
- *Dosage Forms*: Available in 2.5 mg, 5 mg, 10 mg, and 20 mg tablets. Also available as a once-daily low-dose formulation for men who have frequent sexual activity.
- *Best For*: Those who prefer spontaneity in their sexual activity due to its long duration.

Vardenafil (Levitra, Staxyn)

- *Onset and Duration*: Takes effect within 25 to 60 minutes and lasts about 4 to 5 hours.
- *Dosage Forms*: Available in 5 mg, 10 mg, and 20 mg tablets. Staxyn is an orally disintegrating tablet.

- *Best For*: Men who prefer a fast-acting option with the convenience of an orally disintegrating tablet.

Avanafil (Stendra)

- *Onset and Duration*: Starts working in about 15 to 30 minutes and lasts up to 6 hours.
- *Dosage Forms*: Available in 50 mg, 100 mg, and 200 mg tablets.
- *Best For*: Rapid onset and shorter duration make it suitable for spontaneous encounters.

Comparison of Features:

- *Effectiveness*: All PDE5 inhibitors are effective in improving erectile function in men with ED. The choice often depends on individual preferences regarding onset time and duration of action.
- *Side Effects*: Common side effects include headaches, flushing, nasal congestion, indigestion, and dizziness. Visual disturbances are more commonly reported with sildenafil.
- *Food Interactions*: High-fat meals can delay the absorption of sildenafil and vardenafil. Tadalafil and avanafil are less affected by food.

Alternative Therapies and Lifestyle Changes

For some men, ED may be managed or improved with alternative therapies and lifestyle changes, either alone or in conjunction with medication.

Lifestyle Changes

- Exercise: Regular physical activity can improve blood flow, reduce stress, and enhance overall well-being. Aerobic exercises, such as walking, jogging, and cycling, are particularly beneficial.
- *Diet*: A healthy diet rich in fruits, vegetables, whole grains, and lean proteins can improve cardiovascular health and reduce the risk of ED. Foods high in flavonoids, like berries and dark chocolate, have been associated with a reduced risk of ED.
- *Weight Management*: Maintaining a healthy weight can improve erectile function and reduce the risk of cardiovascular diseases that contribute to ED.
- *Smoking Cessation*: Smoking can damage blood vessels and reduce blood flow to the penis. Quitting smoking can improve erectile function.
- *Limit Alcohol*: Excessive alcohol consumption can lead to ED. Moderation is key to minimizing its impact on sexual health.

Psychological Counseling

- *Therapy for Psychological Factors*: Stress, anxiety, and depression can contribute to ED. Counseling or therapy can help address these issues, improve sexual confidence, and enhance relationships.
- *Couples Therapy*: Involving partners in therapy can improve communication and address relationship issues contributing to ED.

Herbal and Natural Remedies

- *Ginseng*: Some studies suggest that Panax ginseng may improve erectile function, but more research is needed.
- *L-Arginine*: An amino acid that may improve blood flow to the penis by increasing nitric oxide levels. It may be beneficial for some men, but its effectiveness varies.

Medical Devices

- Vacuum Erection Devices (VEDs): These devices use vacuum pressure to draw blood into the penis, inducing an erection. They can be effective for men who cannot take PDE5 inhibitors.

- Penile Implants: Surgically implanted devices can provide a permanent solution for ED. They are usually considered when other treatments have failed.

Combination Therapies

Combination of PDE5 Inhibitors with Other Treatments

- *Low-Dose Daily Tadalafil with On-Demand Sildenafil*: Some men benefit from combining a daily low-dose PDE5 inhibitor with an on-demand PDE5 inhibitor to enhance erectile function.
- *PDE5 Inhibitors and Vacuum Devices*: Using a vacuum erection device alongside medication can enhance the erection quality.

Hormone Replacement Therapy

- *Testosterone Replacement Therapy (TRT)*: For men with low testosterone levels, TRT may improve libido and erectile function when used alongside PDE5 inhibitors.

Lifestyle Changes and Medications

- Adopting lifestyle changes such as diet, exercise, and smoking cessation while using ED medications can maximize effectiveness and improve overall health.

Viagra and other ED treatments offer various options for managing erectile dysfunction. The choice of therapy depends on individual needs, preferences, and underlying health conditions. Consulting with a healthcare provider can help determine the best treatment plan. In the next chapter, we will discuss the importance of consulting with a healthcare provider and the role of personalized treatment plans for erectile dysfunction.

Chapter 8: Psychological and Relationship Aspects

Erectile dysfunction (ED) is not only a physical condition but also one that can have significant psychological and relationship impacts. Understanding these aspects is crucial for effectively managing ED and improving quality of life.

The Impact of ED on Mental Health

Erectile dysfunction can profoundly affect a man's mental health, contributing to a range of emotional and psychological challenges.

Anxiety and Stress

- *Performance Anxiety*: Men with ED often experience anxiety about their ability to perform sexually. This stress can exacerbate the condition, creating a vicious cycle.

- *General Stress*: The stress of living with ED can spill over into other areas of life, affecting work, social interactions, and overall well-being.

Depression

- *Feelings of Inadequacy*: ED can lead to feelings of inadequacy, shame, and low self-esteem. These feelings can contribute to or worsen depression.
- *Loss of Interest*: Men with ED may lose interest in sexual activity due to fear of failure, leading to withdrawal from intimacy and further contributing to depressive symptoms.

Impact on Self-Esteem

- *Body Image Concerns*: Concerns about body image and masculinity can be intensified by ED. The inability to maintain an erection may lead to feelings of decreased masculinity.
- *Confidence Issues*: A decline in self-esteem and confidence can impact social interactions and professional life.

Emotional Withdrawal

- *Avoidance of Intimacy*: Men with ED may avoid intimate situations, fearing embarrassment or failure, which can lead to emotional distancing from partners.
- *Social Isolation*: Withdrawal from social situations and activities due to feelings of inadequacy or depression can lead to isolation.

Communication with Partners

Open and honest communication with a partner is essential in managing the relationship impact of ED.

Discussing the Condition

- *Honesty:* Being honest with your partner about the condition can relieve tension and reduce misunderstandings.
- *Sharing Feelings*: Expressing feelings of frustration, anxiety, or embarrassment can help partners understand the emotional impact of ED.

Addressing Misunderstandings

- *Clarifying Misconceptions*: Partners may mistakenly believe that ED is a sign of reduced attraction or infidelity. Addressing these misconceptions can prevent unnecessary conflict.
- *Reassurance:* Providing reassurance that ED is a medical condition and not a reflection of the relationship's quality can help maintain emotional closeness.

Exploring Solutions Together

- *Joint Problem Solving*: Involving the partner in exploring treatment options and lifestyle changes can foster a sense of teamwork and support.
- *Experimenting with Alternatives*: Couples can explore non-penetrative forms of intimacy to maintain a satisfying sexual relationship.

Setting Realistic Expectations

- *Patience*: Understanding that treatment and recovery take time can reduce pressure and stress.
- *Flexibility*: Being open to different approaches and adapting to changes in sexual function can enhance relationship satisfaction.

Counseling and Support Options

Seeking professional help can be beneficial for both individuals and couples dealing with the psychological aspects of ED.

Individual Therapy

- *Cognitive Behavioral Therapy (CBT)*: CBT can help address negative thought patterns and behaviors associated with ED, reducing anxiety and depression.
- *Stress Management Techniques*: Learning stress management techniques, such as mindfulness and relaxation exercises, can help alleviate anxiety related to sexual performance.

Couples Therapy

- *Improving Communication*: Couples therapy can improve communication skills, helping partners to express feelings and needs more effectively.
- *Rebuilding Intimacy*: Therapists can guide couples in rebuilding emotional and physical intimacy, focusing on non-sexual forms of connection.

Support Groups

- *Peer Support*: Joining support groups can provide a sense of community and understanding from others facing similar challenges.
- *Sharing Experiences*: Sharing experiences and solutions with others can reduce feelings of isolation and offer new perspectives.

Online Resources and Education

- *Educational Materials*: Accessing educational materials about ED can empower individuals and couples with knowledge about the condition and treatment options.
- *Online Forums*: Participating in online forums can provide a space for anonymous discussion and support.

Understanding the psychological and relationship aspects of ED is crucial for comprehensive management of the condition. Open communication, counseling, and support can help individuals and couples navigate the challenges of ED, improving mental health and relationship satisfaction.

Chapter 9: Practical Tips for Users

For individuals using Viagra or other treatments for erectile dysfunction (ED), maximizing effectiveness and managing expectations is essential for achieving the best outcomes. This chapter provides practical tips for users, focusing on enhancing the effectiveness of treatment, managing expectations, and dealing with anxiety and performance pressure.

How to Maximize Effectiveness

Maximizing the effectiveness of Viagra involves understanding how to use it correctly and optimizing the conditions for its use.

Follow Prescribed Dosage and Timing

- *Adhere to Prescribed Dosage*: Always follow the healthcare provider's prescribed dosage and instructions. Do not adjust the dose without consulting a doctor.
- *Timing:* Take Viagra about 30 to 60 minutes before sexual activity. Plan accordingly to allow the medication time to work.

Avoid Large or High-Fat Meals

- *Impact on Absorption*: Large or high-fat meals can delay Viagra’s absorption, making it less effective. Consider taking Viagra on an empty stomach or after a light meal.

Limit Alcohol Consumption

- *Alcohol Interaction*: Excessive alcohol can reduce Viagra’s effectiveness and increase the risk of side effects such as dizziness and headaches. Limit alcohol intake when planning to use Viagra.

Stay Hydrated

- *Hydration*: Drink plenty of water to ensure proper hydration, as dehydration can impact overall bodily functions, including sexual performance.

Combine with Healthy Lifestyle Choices

- *Exercise Regularly*: Regular physical activity can improve cardiovascular health, enhance blood flow, and boost erectile function.
- *Healthy Diet*: A balanced diet rich in fruits, vegetables, whole grains, and lean proteins can support overall health and erectile function.

Manage Underlying Health Conditions

- *Chronic Conditions*: Control conditions like diabetes, hypertension, and high cholesterol, as these can affect erectile function. Work with a healthcare provider to manage these conditions effectively.

Managing Expectations

Understanding what Viagra can and cannot do is crucial for managing expectations and ensuring a positive experience.

Realistic Expectations

- *Not a Cure*: Viagra is not a cure for ED but a treatment that helps achieve and maintain an erection when sexually stimulated.
- *Variable Response*: Response to Viagra can vary among individuals. It may take a few attempts to find the right dosage and timing for optimal results.

Understand the Duration

- *Duration of Action*: Viagra typically lasts about 4 hours. However, this does not mean a continuous erection; rather, it facilitates erections when sexually aroused within this timeframe.

Communicate with Your Partner

- *Open Dialogue*: Communicate openly with your partner about using Viagra and set realistic expectations about its effects and duration.
- *Involve Your Partner*: Engage your partner in the treatment process, exploring intimacy and non-sexual activities to strengthen your relationship.

Monitor and Adjust

- *Trial and Error*: It may take time to find the optimal approach to using Viagra. Be patient and willing to adjust timing or dosage as needed under a doctor's guidance.

Dealing with Anxiety and Performance Pressure

Anxiety and performance pressure can hinder the effectiveness of Viagra. Learning to manage these feelings is vital for improving outcomes.

3.1. Practice Relaxation Techniques

- *Deep Breathing*: Practice deep breathing exercises to reduce stress and anxiety before sexual activity.
- *Mindfulness and Meditation*: Engage in mindfulness or meditation practices to focus on the present moment and reduce anxiety.

Address Psychological Barriers

- *Seek Counseling:* Consider individual or couples counseling to address underlying psychological issues contributing to ED.
- *Cognitive Behavioral Therapy (CBT)*: CBT can help change negative thought patterns related to sexual performance and improve self-confidence.

Focus on Intimacy, Not Just Performance

- *Non-Sexual Intimacy*: Engage in activities that promote intimacy and closeness, such as cuddling, kissing, or massages, to reduce performance pressure.
- *Shift Focus*: Focus on the pleasure and connection rather than solely on achieving an erection or reaching orgasm.

Set Realistic Goals

- *Incremental Progress*: Set small, achievable goals for sexual encounters rather than striving for perfection each time.
- *Celebrate Successes*: Recognize and celebrate improvements and successes, however small, to build confidence and reduce anxiety.

Support and Encouragement

- *Partner Support*: Encourage open communication with your partner, seeking their support and reassurance to alleviate anxiety.
- *Peer Support*: Consider joining support groups where you can share experiences and gain insights from others facing similar challenges.

By implementing these practical tips, users of Viagra can maximize the medication's effectiveness, manage their expectations, and reduce anxiety and performance pressure. A holistic approach that combines medical treatment with lifestyle changes and psychological support can lead to improved outcomes and a more satisfying sexual experience.

Chapter 10: Future of ED Treatments

The field of erectile dysfunction (ED) treatment is evolving rapidly, with ongoing research and development aiming to enhance existing therapies and introduce innovative solutions. This chapter explores the future of ED treatments, focusing on advances in research, new medications and therapies in development, and the role of personalized medicine in managing ED.

Advances in ED Research

Scientific advancements continue to shed light on the underlying mechanisms of erectile dysfunction, paving the way for novel treatment approaches.

Understanding the Molecular Pathways

- *Nitric Oxide Pathway*: Researchers are exploring deeper into the role of nitric oxide (NO) and cyclic guanosine monophosphate (cGMP) in the erectile process. Understanding these pathways may lead to the development of drugs that target these mechanisms more precisely.
- *Neurovascular Interactions*: Studies on the interaction between the nervous and vascular systems in the context of erections are expanding. Insights into these interactions could help in developing treatments that address both psychological and physiological aspects of ED.

Gene and Stem Cell Therapy

- *Gene Therapy:* Research is underway to develop gene therapy approaches that target specific genetic factors contributing to ED. This could involve introducing or modifying genes to enhance erectile function.
- *Stem Cell Therapy*: Early studies suggest that stem cells might regenerate damaged tissues and improve erectile function, offering a potential treatment for ED resulting from nerve damage or other injuries.

Advances in Drug Delivery Systems

- *Nanotechnology*: Nanotechnology is being explored to develop more efficient drug delivery systems, ensuring targeted delivery of ED medications with reduced side effects.
- *Transdermal Systems*: Innovative delivery systems such as patches or topical applications are being developed to provide more convenient alternatives to oral medications.

New Medications and Therapies in Development

As research progresses, new medications and therapies are being developed to offer more effective and convenient treatment options for ED.

Next-Generation PDE5 Inhibitors

- *Improved Efficacy*: Researchers are working on next-generation PDE5 inhibitors with enhanced efficacy and fewer side effects. These drugs aim to provide faster onset and longer duration with improved safety profiles.

- *Alternative Formulations*: Development of alternative formulations, such as orally disintegrating tablets or liquid forms, may provide more convenient options for users.

Novel Drug Classes

- *Rho-Kinase Inhibitors*: These drugs target the Rho-kinase pathway involved in penile erection, offering a potential alternative for those who do not respond to PDE5 inhibitors.
- *Melanocortin Receptor Agonists*: This class of drugs works on the central nervous system to enhance sexual arousal and erectile function, representing a different approach to ED treatment.

Shockwave Therapy

- *Low-Intensity Extracorporeal Shockwave Therapy (LI-ESWT)*: This non-invasive therapy uses shockwaves to improve blood flow and promote the regeneration of blood vessels in the penis. It has shown promise in clinical trials and may offer a long-term solution for ED.

Platelet-Rich Plasma (PRP) Therapy

- *Regenerative Approach*: PRP therapy involves injecting platelet-rich plasma derived from the patient's blood into the penis. This therapy aims to promote tissue regeneration and improve erectile function.

Personalized Medicine and ED

Personalized medicine is becoming increasingly important in the treatment of erectile dysfunction, tailoring therapies to individual needs and genetic profiles.

Genetic Profiling

- *Understanding Variability*: Genetic profiling can help identify individual differences in response to ED treatments, enabling more personalized and effective treatment plans.
- *Pharmacogenomics*: Understanding how genetic factors influence drug metabolism and response can guide the selection of the most appropriate medication and dosage for each individual.

Customized Treatment Plans

- *Holistic Approach*: Personalized medicine involves a comprehensive approach that considers lifestyle, psychological factors, and comorbidities, allowing for more tailored treatment strategies.

- *Combination Therapies*: By assessing individual needs and responses, healthcare providers can design combination therapies that address multiple aspects of ED, enhancing overall treatment efficacy.

Patient-Centric Care

- *Informed Decision-Making*: Personalized medicine empowers patients by providing them with information about their unique condition and treatment options, facilitating informed decision-making.
- *Improved Outcomes*: By aligning treatment strategies with individual needs and preferences, personalized medicine aims to improve patient satisfaction and treatment outcomes.

The future of ED treatments is promising, with ongoing research and development efforts focused on providing more effective, convenient, and personalized solutions. As the understanding of the underlying mechanisms of ED expands and new therapies emerge, individuals with erectile dysfunction can look forward to a broader range of options for managing their condition.

Chapter 11: Legal and Ethical Considerations

When it comes to treating erectile dysfunction (ED), understanding the legal and ethical considerations of obtaining and using Viagra is crucial. This chapter covers the importance of obtaining Viagra safely and legally, avoiding counterfeit products, and addressing privacy and confidentiality concerns.

Obtaining Viagra Safely and Legally

Ensuring the safe and legal acquisition of Viagra involves understanding the necessary steps and requirements.

Prescription Requirement

- *Consult a Healthcare Provider*: Viagra is a prescription medication, meaning it should only be obtained through consultation with a qualified healthcare provider. A doctor can assess your condition, recommend the appropriate treatment, and provide a prescription if Viagra is suitable for you.

- *Legitimate Pharmacies*: Fill prescriptions at licensed and legitimate pharmacies, either in-person or online. This ensures you receive authentic and safe medication.

Understanding Regulations

- *Regulatory Approval*: Ensure that the Viagra you purchase is approved by relevant health authorities, such as the U.S. Food and Drug Administration (FDA) or the European Medicines Agency (EMA). Approval indicates that the medication has been tested for safety and efficacy.
- *Country-Specific Regulations*: Be aware of the regulations in your country regarding the purchase and use of prescription medications. Different countries have different rules, and purchasing medication across borders can be illegal or unsafe.

Online Purchases

- *Reputable Online Pharmacies*: If purchasing Viagra online, use reputable pharmacies that require a valid prescription. Legitimate online pharmacies often display

certification seals from recognized organizations, such as the National Association of Boards of Pharmacy (NABP) in the United States.
- *Avoiding Unverified Websites*: Be cautious of websites offering Viagra without a prescription or at significantly reduced prices, as these are often illegal and may sell counterfeit products.

Avoiding Counterfeit Products

Counterfeit medications pose serious health risks and avoiding them is essential for safety.

Risks of Counterfeit Viagra

- *Ineffectiveness:* Counterfeit Viagra may not contain the active ingredient sildenafil, making it ineffective in treating ED.
- *Potential Harm*: Counterfeit drugs can contain harmful substances, incorrect dosages, or contaminants, posing significant health risks.

Identifying Counterfeit Products

- *Packaging and Appearance*: Authentic Viagra packaging includes holograms, batch numbers, and expiry dates. Counterfeit products may have misspelled labels, incorrect logos, or unusual colors and shapes.
- *Price Discrepancies:* Be wary of prices that seem too good to be true, as they may indicate counterfeit products. Viagra is a premium medication, and prices that are significantly lower than average should raise suspicion.

Reporting Counterfeit Products

- *Health Authorities*: Report suspected counterfeit Viagra to local health authorities or regulatory bodies. This helps authorities take action against illegal operations and protect public health.
- *Pharmaceutical Companies*: Inform the manufacturer, Pfizer, if you encounter counterfeit products. They have measures in place to address such issues and protect consumers.

Privacy and Confidentiality Concerns

Maintaining privacy and confidentiality is a critical aspect of managing ED and obtaining Viagra.

Patient Confidentiality

- *Doctor-Patient Confidentiality*: Healthcare providers are bound by confidentiality agreements, ensuring that your medical information, including your ED diagnosis and treatment, is kept private.
- *Trustworthy Providers*: Choose healthcare providers and pharmacies that prioritize patient privacy and adhere to data protection laws, such as the Health Insurance Portability and Accountability Act (HIPAA) in the United States or the General Data Protection Regulation (GDPR) in Europe.

Discreet Transactions

- *Discreet Packaging*: Many pharmacies offer discreet packaging for Viagra deliveries to protect your privacy.
- *Secure Online Transactions*: Use secure websites and payment methods when purchasing Viagra online to protect your financial and personal information.

Online Data Protection

- *Data Security*: Ensure that online pharmacies use encryption and other security measures to protect your personal data during transactions.

- *Awareness of Scams*: Be cautious of phishing scams or unsolicited emails offering ED medications, as these can compromise your privacy and financial security.

Understanding the legal and ethical considerations surrounding Viagra use is crucial for ensuring safe and effective treatment. By obtaining Viagra through legitimate channels, avoiding counterfeit products, and protecting your privacy, you can manage ED responsibly and securely.

Chapter 12: FAQs and User Stories

In this chapter, we will address some of the most frequently asked questions about Viagra and share experiences and testimonials from users. These insights aim to provide a comprehensive understanding of the medication and its impact on those who use it.

Common Questions Answered

1. **How long does Viagra take to work?**

Viagra typically begins to work within 30 to 60 minutes after ingestion. However, it requires sexual arousal to be effective. The onset time can vary depending on factors such as the user's metabolism, overall health, and whether it was taken on an empty stomach.

2. **How long does the effect of Viagra last?**

The effects of Viagra can last for about four to five hours. This does not mean a continuous erection for this duration but rather the ability to achieve and maintain an erection when sexually stimulated. Individual experiences may vary.

3. **Can I take Viagra with alcohol?**

While moderate alcohol consumption may not significantly affect Viagra's efficacy, excessive alcohol can impair its effectiveness and increase the risk of side effects such as dizziness and headaches. It is best to limit alcohol intake when using Viagra.

4. **Can I take Viagra every day?**

Viagra is usually taken as needed and should not be taken more than once in a 24-hour period. For those who anticipate frequent sexual activity, a healthcare provider may suggest other ED medications designed for daily use. Always follow your doctor's recommendations regarding dosage and frequency.

5. **What should I do if Viagra doesn't work?**

If Viagra does not work the first time, it is important not to give up immediately. Sometimes, finding the right dose or timing can make a difference. Consult your healthcare provider if Viagra is consistently ineffective, as they may adjust the dose or recommend alternative treatments.

6. Are there any long-term effects of taking Viagra?

When used as prescribed, Viagra is generally safe for long-term use. However, it is important to have regular check-ups with a healthcare provider to monitor for any potential side effects or interactions with other medications.

7. Can women take Viagra?

Viagra is not approved for use in women, and its safety and efficacy in women have not been established. Some studies are exploring its effects on women, particularly for female sexual arousal disorders, but these are not conclusive yet.

8. Can young men take Viagra?

Viagra is prescribed for adult men diagnosed with erectile dysfunction, regardless of age. However, young men should only use it if prescribed by a healthcare provider, as unnecessary use can lead to psychological dependence and mask underlying health issues.

Experiences and Testimonials from Users

User stories provide valuable insights into the personal impact of Viagra on individuals and their relationships. Here are some experiences shared by users:

- **Mark's Story**

Mark, a 58-year-old engineer, began experiencing ED due to diabetes. Initially hesitant, he consulted his doctor and started using Viagra. "Viagra has been a game-changer for me. It restored my confidence and brought back the intimacy in my marriage. I was worried about side effects, but I only experienced mild headaches, which were manageable."

- **Sarah and Tom's Experience**

Tom, aged 65, struggled with ED after heart surgery. With his wife Sarah's support, he sought medical advice and was prescribed Viagra. "We were apprehensive about using medication, but Viagra helped restore our relationship. We learned to communicate better, and the pressure was off knowing we had a reliable solution," Sarah shared.

- **Alex's Journey**

Alex, a 42-year-old teacher, experienced performance anxiety that affected his erectile function. After discussing with his doctor, he used Viagra alongside cognitive behavioral therapy. "Viagra helped me realize that my issues were more about anxiety than a physical problem. It gave me the boost I needed while I worked on my anxiety."

- **Mike's Insights**

Mike, 50, was concerned about taking Viagra due to high blood pressure. After consulting with his healthcare provider, he was given the all-clear to use it safely. "Viagra helped me regain control over my sex life. It was important to speak openly with my doctor about my concerns, and I'm glad I did."

- **Jane and David's Perspective**

David, 55, faced ED due to prostate cancer treatment. Jane, his partner, was supportive throughout the process. "Viagra wasn't just about restoring erections; it was about bringing intimacy back into our lives. It required patience and understanding, but it improved our relationship in unexpected ways," Jane noted.

These user stories highlight the diverse experiences with Viagra, emphasizing the importance of consulting healthcare providers and maintaining open communication with partners. While Viagra is an effective solution for many, each individual's journey is unique, and the medication's impact can vary. Understanding personal experiences can help others make informed decisions and foster supportive conversations about ED and its treatment.

Conclusion

Erectile dysfunction (ED) is a prevalent condition affecting millions of men worldwide, with significant impacts on physical health, mental well-being, and intimate relationships. Viagra, a pioneering medication for ED, has transformed the lives of countless individuals by providing a reliable and effective treatment option. As we've explored in this guide, understanding the multifaceted aspects of Viagra and its use is essential for maximizing its benefits and ensuring safe and effective treatment.

Recap of Key Points

1. **Understanding Erectile Dysfunction**

- *Causes and Prevalence*: ED can result from a range of physical, psychological, and lifestyle factors. Understanding these causes is essential for effective treatment and management.

- *Impact on Mental Health and Relationships*: ED can lead to stress, anxiety, and strained relationships. Addressing these aspects is as important as treating the physical symptoms.

2. **Viagra: Mechanism and Usage**

- *Mechanism of Action*: Viagra works by enhancing blood flow to the penis, facilitating the achievement and maintenance of an erection when sexually stimulated.
- *Usage Guidelines*: Proper dosage, timing, and lifestyle considerations can maximize Viagra's effectiveness and minimize potential side effects.

3. **Safety and Side Effects**

- *Common Side Effects*: While generally well-tolerated, Viagra can cause headaches, flushing, and dizziness. Understanding these potential side effects helps users manage them effectively.
- *Contraindications and Interactions*: Certain health conditions and medications can contraindicate the use of Viagra. Consulting a healthcare provider is crucial to ensure safe use.

4. Legal and Ethical Considerations

- *Obtaining Viagra Legally*: Always acquire Viagra through legitimate channels to avoid counterfeit products and ensure safety.
- *Privacy Concerns*: Protecting patient confidentiality and data security is essential when seeking treatment for ED.

5. Future of ED Treatments

- *Innovative Therapies*: Advances in research are paving the way for new medications and therapies, offering hope for more effective and personalized treatments.
- *Personalized Medicine*: Tailoring treatment plans to individual needs and genetic profiles can enhance outcomes and patient satisfaction.

6. Psychological and Relationship Aspects

- *Communication and Support*: Open dialogue with partners and seeking counseling can improve relationships and reduce the psychological burden of ED.

Encouragement for Safe and Informed Use

Using Viagra safely and effectively requires informed decision-making and responsible use. Here are some key points to consider:

- *Consult Healthcare Professionals*: Always seek medical advice before starting Viagra or any ED treatment. A healthcare provider can assess your condition, recommend the appropriate dosage, and monitor for any potential interactions or side effects.
- *Follow Prescribed Guidelines*: Adhere to the prescribed dosage and timing and make lifestyle adjustments as recommended by your healthcare provider to enhance effectiveness and safety.
- *Monitor Health and Well-being*: Regular check-ups and open communication with your doctor can help address any concerns and ensure that your treatment remains safe and effective.
- *Avoid Unregulated Sources*: Obtain Viagra from legitimate sources only to ensure authenticity and safety. Be cautious of counterfeit products, especially when purchasing online.

Resources for Further Information and Support

To support individuals dealing with ED, numerous resources are available:

- *Healthcare Providers*: Consult your doctor or a specialist for personalized advice and treatment options.
- *Educational Websites*: Trusted medical websites like Mayo Clinic, WebMD, and the National Institutes of Health (NIH) offer valuable information about ED and its treatments.
- *Support Groups*: Online forums and local support groups provide platforms for individuals to share experiences and seek advice from peers.
- *Counseling Services*: Professional counseling can help address psychological and relational aspects of ED, offering guidance and support for both individuals and couples.

By understanding the complexities of ED and Viagra, individuals can make informed choices that enhance their health and well-being. This guide aims to empower readers with the knowledge necessary to navigate their ED journey confidently and responsibly, seeking the support and resources needed for a fulfilling and healthy life.

www.ingramcontent.com/pod-product-compliance
Lightning Source LLC
LaVergne TN
LVHW010730090726
842905LV00040B/995